Burnout Diary

Poems by

Abby Hosterman

Burnout Diary

ISBN: 979-8-9924550-0-7

Cover art by Catherine Weiss.

Edited by Devin Devine.

www.gameoverbooks.com

Overfunctional

When I am sick, I am not.

At my daughter's french fry science fair
project, I am secretly gut-punched with the loss.
I am who they created participation awards for.

On the gynecologist's crinkle paper
and going through TSA and in line
to scan my library books back in,
I hope no one notices how hard I am trying
to be the best.

My therapist tells me "B is bravo"
and the only time I've lied to her is with a nod,
my fingers crossed into an A+
behind my back.

Am I getting fired?

Remember when I took the work call
dilating on the birthing ball?

The thing about being born in August
is it can go one of two ways and I go both,
so I don't miss a thing.

My wildest fantasy is being
in multiple places at once. I can do it
if I give myself no other choice.

Burnout
is like a dozen eggs, a month's supply
of painkillers from the dentist,
it's simply how they come.

Once someone told me
they were disappointed in me.
It was my mother.

Once a bell rang
and nothing absorbed the noise
so it vibrated forever.

Turns out, participation is not required.
Turns out,
I am finite.

The Motherwound: A Birthday Poem

It is almost her birthday
and I am trying to turn it into a poem
again. If you see her, tell her

I am wishing her the best.
Tell her I do not have time to write
this poem again, but I am trying

for the tenth time. I am fitting it in,
it won't fit out. Tell her I woke up this morning
and my heart is full, but of termites with her face.

Tell her I am puzzled. I've been
told that it cannot be held against me
that I was a child when I was a child.

On your mother's birthday, tell her
you are thankful that she was born.
On my mother's birthday, I'm asking

to be told you are thankful that I was.

Birthright

You don't know what you
don't know except what you know
from your mother's bones.

Regret is A Nest That Holds Me

People are going to think I'm a serial killer.
My grandfather kept a sign
in the front of his print shop that said
"FRESH EGGS, JUST ASK"
he would pay me a dollar to fetch them
from the chickens. The birds recognized
the recycled styrofoam cartons, thought
I came with corn or a stale doughnut,
scratched towards me—evolved little dinosaurs,
all beak and ego and beady eyed zig zag
clucking; how we, my sister *and* I,
took a two by four with us into the coop
to knock the birds off their shit feathered seed
when it was our turn to collect; how I found out
years later that I was the only one who took
a two by four with me, that my sister gasped
and threw up her two innocent hands
when she heard what I had done, how I am trying
to stop regretting not knowing better
how to protect myself, how I have so many choices
I am not proud of and do not know whose idea it was
to first hand me a stick.

Imposter Syndrome at The Zoo

I stand the stillest,
but there must be a rumor
that I am desperate.

Butterflies hardly
land on me. I wonder if
they taste that I'm bad.

The less I am loved
the more I will try to show
how much I offer.

Giver

The pearly henge of a cryptid snarl
behind my polite smile, I am

accidentally trying to be more kind
in the interest of not tearing
holes in dough.

There are bushels of apples
popping blood vessels in my cheeks.
I still think there is plenty to go around,

that I am not pie. I am starting to suspect
that I might be wrong.
Aspiring to be infinite is a curse.

Where I end
and the rest begins
is always an outstretched hand,

always a *yes, a will this make my mother proud
if she hears through the grapevine?*
I have heard that there are givers

and takers and I am a red carpet
lined with
let me tie your shoe.

Sour

My mother, the librarian, the poet,
the ruler with a fist of chewed-down fingernails,
had Billy Collins over for dinner in 2002
when he was the National Poet Laureate. When he left
our table, she stashed his lip-printed glass on a shelf
like a snowglobe; joked about saving the toilet paper rolls
but it wasn't a joke. What I am saying is that my mother
liked keeping things, except

when I got my period, it was my grandmother's birthday
and she announced it at dinner.

When she found
my Planned Parenthood receipt, she made charcuterie
for the confrontation.

When I looked for myself
in my father, she curdled and soured
and I haven't heard from her since.

Keeping things does not run through my veins.
Not secrets, not heart, not milk.

Eureka

Laying in bed and it hits me
like a sack of peach pits
swung top speed.

Remember when I fell in love?
How I was swallowed by the risk
of it all? Determined to be

unbelievable? That is what keeps me
fucked up on the mortality
of my hometown. Everyone here

feeds people. They talk about
neighborhoods like they are cities,
talk about cities like they are places

people only visit. My children
are growing up, my grandmother
is growing older, my mother and I

keep growing further apart
while everyone in this town grows
into each other the way a dog

adopts the face of its owner
and I grow hungry, rise
into a piece of the skyline.

First Christmas

Six months pregnant
and the present he got me
came with no box,
no card, no disclaimers.
It crossed my mind
that it may have been stolen
from Good Stuff Thrift:
a retired nail salon lotion warmer
the cord wrapped
like the gift was;
trailing on the floor
as he handed it to me
on Christmas Eve
because he couldn't wait
a second more.
"To warm your lotion
so you stay on top of
the stretch marks!"
he encouraged
with his eyelids high
and his heart
saying all that it knew
how to. I thought
he was being so nice.
He was thoughtful
for all the wrong reasons.
I had been taught
it's the thought
that counts.

Brunch

Apron bow tied tight on broken rib,
neither house, nor wife,
with my one unsprained wrist,

I unflip the couch and arrange it
like a trimmed flower delivery
on the unvacuumed carpet

before the rescue friends arrive
to the He Finally Went Too Far Party.
They pass by the doorbell

and the bouquets of finger in the drywall,
the blood petals that lead up the aisle of stairs
and the sharp smile of the knife

that pirouetted on the floor last night,
a mouthy ballerina, her braced teeth kiss,
the worst game of spin the bottle ever played,

and with their arms full of sympathy
casseroles they say, "It's a new recipe,
so sorry if it sucks."

I greet them at the table
and guide them with my swollen lips
into champagne laughter.

It is so fucking stereotypical
that I defended myself with a frying pan.

His skull grew a clementine. I bent backwards like an elbow. He told me he
would tell the police I was the menace. I believed his rabid hiss, "You spread
your thighs like hotel breakfast." He said it like a secret. His eyes were bigger
than his own face. I tried to call 9-1-1. He shoved the phone in my mouth like a
battered spoon. I tasted blood from the split. They tell you to scream *fire* instead
of *help* but that doesn't work either. If a tree falls in a cul de sac of run down
duplexes and yells *rape*,

no one even comes to the window. The sliding glass door locked me out while
he told me, "Calm the fuck down." My bones would have splintered if I had
jumped off the balcony. I considered it still.

I notice my own echo in the halls
of their pity and origami a napkin
into an apology on my plate: "Sorry. Anyway,"
I take a sip, "He owes me a new frying pan."

And we have to laugh.
But when the silence sets back in
and the rescue friends
have all gone home,

I lose count
of how many times
I've checked the locks.
I ice my aching swell,

hang up my apron,
wipe down the table,
and with the last shred
of woman left in me,

take pride
in what a good host
I've been.

Heard v. Depp

Nothing surprises me
about the way people sided with Johnny
because they liked pirates. They called Amber

"rehearsed testimony" and honestly, it probably was.
She has probably retold the first time he slapped her across the face
hundreds of times, no consent from her own internal dialogue,

shampoo and tears in her eyes. I could win an Oscar
for the first time I was hit undeniably on purpose. The parked car
in the lot of Asbury Lanes, the erratic driving, the way the singer scowled

at his cigarette breath yelling so loud over the music that I became all black-eyed
spiders of embarrassment. I could do a musical number about being a kickline floor.
The anchorman says "she has to prove that she's been abused."

She has a video of him,
Edward Bottle of Wine Hands,
and instead they asked
"why'd she press record?"

and he made them laugh until question marks popped like tiny bubbles
in the courtroom parade and all the people were dotted with his spit.
Little jokes.
Little man.

When they roll the tape, the jury closes its eyes tight and imagines
their favorite movie. Being attacked turned me feral, turned a gentle woman
into fang. When he held me down by the pubic bone and ruined my birthday,

changed my name to Dog Shit, I wiped the foam from my mouth
and wore the right skirt. Why didn't she leave? Trust me,
when a bystander tells you that you are not safe, you don't want to believe them
because who would believe you back? There is a woman on TV

trying to prove that a man who said "I'll peel your fucking hair back"
is guilty of abuse. I told a mandatory reporter in my abuser's family on Christ-
mas Eve
and she told me,
"I don't think so."

The first time I took a photo of a bruise, I was trying
to convince myself. Let me promise: at some point,
you gotta hit back. At some point, my days were numbered
airport terminal lawless. I lost access to the weather.
I turned your fingernails into a part of my palm, knew
how wide my mouth could stretch before it ripped at the seams.
Everyone asks for evidence while you are just standing there.

Holy mother of his strangle, your honor
in doubt, bad lighting on your fingerprint neck, and
his good word.

The Year That a Song Called Happy Was Number One

All hammer, no nail; that year, I didn't throw caution to the wind,
I threw it to the cyclone. I was the worst house in the neighborhood.
While everyone else was throwing block parties with bubble wands

and baby pools, I was drawing the blinds and braiding friendship
bracelets with the ashtrays, beading white cubes with black letters
into the names of men who were stringing me along, men

I had imagined wanted to go for breakfast with me who definitely did
not. I convinced myself I would not want to forget them and I absolutely
did. I called on women with reckless emotion and they sent me to voicemail

at 5AM again. My mother returned to sender every letter. All of the grass died.
I piled locks on the doors. The eviction notices kept coming from inside of me—
their official lipstick print screaming from the mailbox of my own mouth.

I threw them up onto a pile of unpaid bills, the snowballing late fees, takeout menus.
In all of 2014, I don't think I opened a single envelope. Lost the mail key.
I couldn't bear the paper cuts on top of everything else. I had ruined myself

enough that the thrill was gone. With nowhere to go and no one to help,
I learned to lift from my unpraying kneecaps, to sit on a therapist's couch,
to spackle all of the blackholes in my memory with ink and a magnifying glass.

People who hate you can act like they don't. There is no revenge sweet enough
to hang in your hallway. I bought a calendar and wrote my name in every box.

Honey

The most beautiful thing I have ever heard is: my best friend
was 12 and at sleepaway camp when she got her period

for the first time: her curls cramping tight in the stall,
dark wood always damp from the shower caddies. I wish I could know

every woman in my life as they were when they were girls. I have
never wanted to be kissed more than when I was a girl and had no idea

what I would do if I was, the possibility still unrealistic. Summers
by the boombox on the bean bag with the notebook of song lyrics

I wrote down by ear, Savage Garden on my elbows. To be a girl was to be
in love with everything except myself but only because I hardly even knew

I existed, in a way like being free. All there was was the whole world,
all there was was everyone else, a puzzle with the edges put together,

unaware that pieces could be missing from the guts. Girlhood
was a friendship bracelet we made for ourselves when we hadn't met

yet, the kind you have to cut to take off. Tell me about your girlhood
like you are saying a prayer and you are the altar, the virgin, the baby, you are.

Back when watermelons still had seeds that sprouted into fruit bellies, before
I knew *knuckle*, I remember the summer like it was honey. Tell me

about your girlhood. Let me tell you about mine. Let's meet each other
there in the stickiness; us girls.

LDR

I used to love you so much that I would forget
to fill up my gas tank, sat on the side of Route 1

and looked at your photo;
never slept,

was never tired;
never ate,

was only offered pretzels
on airplanes.

When I did doze off, phone on my chest,
I awoke to an alarm clock recalling your mouth.

I was recently asked how old I was
and all I could remember was your shoe size

and all I could dream of was walking through the night
to wave back at you from across the street.

My mailbox's cheeks full of your tshirts
after your suitcase was folded perfectly into a frown.

I used to love you in a language I didn't know
I could write on the bathroom mirror. Still do.

Gestalt

All I know about
grief sat there across from me
on a leather chair.

Nightmare Where I Attend My Estranged Mother's Dinner Party

With the last drop of gas in my bank account,
I arrive in a new sweater with a box of Camel Lights.
See, I know her.

The door swerves open its arms and I crash in, hot honey spice in the air,
the dogs are barking. She is a dog person now which I already knew
from Googling her new life with my sister. Above the fireplace,

there is a painting she had commissioned after the last divorce
of herself wearing a suit of armor, riding an exotic cat
over an active volcano; my mother

got all of the art because he was tired of arguing, never looked
at it again. A person takes my jacket and they do not have a face
because I do not know the people who know her anymore.

I am offered a seat that is inching obediently towards the garbage.
There is nowhere for me to set my tap shoes. I was afraid
my guts would feel like this again. I used to hide in the closet

like a crushed board game and call it *playing*.
I walk by the kitchen and hear my second father's buttons
rattling indignantly in the utensil drawer.

At the table I pull out Gestalt's empty chair and my therapist
tells me to speak to it as if it is my mother, sit in it and respond
as if I am. I make room for half of myself in the champagne bucket.

There are too many lights in the dining room for her
to come to the table– head pounding to the orange glow
of the empty white-capped bottles. Barney the Dinosaur brings her

a pot and a spoon and before it touches her yellowed lips,
she says that I am rotten and she has never been greater.
Even worse, Olivia Benson asks her if she is here and she gets to say yes,

knows I am well-trained in following her lead,
acts soft-boiled, builds a new best friend
from hourglass sand, beams them up

while she ties their shoelaces together with her tentacles.
I think to myself, *are you new here to the mothership?*
She is vibrating with the satisfaction of them not knowing

better and the ice clinks in the good crystal. She inhales,
taps a cigarette cherry to the candy dish ashtray
I fired in the elementary art class kiln, sets a syringe

to a vinyl record of a dial tone, hisses *this has to be
the greatest dinner party* she has ever thrown, then
snarls me back out the door.

Low Rise Jeans

In the nineties, there were diet chips called WOW! Chips
that were rumored to give people anal leakage, but women
hated themselves enough to take the risk and now my generation

is shackled to the belief that we can't wear dangly earrings
due to the length of our necks. Joke's on you. A woman will always be
my muse: her conversation, her generosity, her mother's spite.

To be a woman's friend is a holy matrimony. The more I talk to women,
the more I learn that I can have, the less I have to tolerate.
No wonder they want us

all to shut up.

Hometown

I've left better places than you, but here I am
writing you a love letter.

You know pull-your-hair-out love?

The kind of love that locks your jaw,
turns your teeth to broken glass?

When I was unlearning, I still showed up

on your stoops.
And now, I roll my eyes at your name

but I still think about you,

still think about the leaves in October,
the trail in the Spring.

After I Have Told a Secret That I Didn't Ask To Keep

There is no good time to wake up; dry mouthed

from a vulnerability hangover, still gutted sore

from my own sword, the static is more static.

I am pretending to be a person who goes to the dentist

and puts gas in the car and checks the bank account

and sends a birthday card and why do men misbehave?

When I've been stung by a hive of bees one at a time

and now I'm dry heaving an apology and showing up

covered in calamine lotion, but still showing up

like I always do. I want to be Mother, want to be Good Job,

want to make my mother proud. Cancel with the dentist.

I don't need the car to lay in the bathtub, driving the faucet

with my feet to the right water temperature, keep simmering

until my body becomes broth. Feed myself to myself,

I cannot afford not to. There is a clock perspiring on the wall

even though it has done nothing wrong.

Winning Therapy

My husband's therapist says he can cut back
 to every other week if he wants, and I say,
"Ohhh… *so you won therapy.*"

I tell my therapist this and she laughs.
When I make my therapist laugh
so hard she cries, it means that I *won* therapy.
Whenever I mention him winning therapy, she laughs
so hard she cries, so I win therapy

every time.

My therapist says she is traveling next week
and I say, "so I'm not gonna see you until the week after?"
and she says I'm fine to not see her until the week after,
I'm doing well. And I say, "so I won?"

She laughs.
I win.

Sometimes I go to therapy
and tell my therapist how good I am doing
and I really believe myself only to come home
and swallow myself whole a few days later
which makes me wonder if I'm actually ever really good
or if I'm just really good at pretending I am.

I decide in the bathtub that the next time I go to therapy,
        two Fridays from now since I don't have to go next week
                because I'm doing so well,
                        I am going to tell my therapist
about how I feel guilty when anyone is kind to me
        and that might be a good place to start
                when I'm healed
                        and done with all my mom shit.

Does acting up when anyone is nice to me or rescheduling
        every appointment since she told me she is grateful
            that I never cancel mean something?
                    Being a person anyone is grateful for feels like lying.
The late night deep dives and throat lumps when
        anyone believes in me, the fact that I think about everything
            that has ever happened to me
                everyday might mean something.

But, not next week.
        I'm not going to therapy next week

        because I'm doing so well.

Trying Mindfulness

Oh no, here comes my brain

knocking again, a herd of carolers
singing a chorus of hypotheticals;

last time I ruined my night like this

it all worked out eventually.
I want to microdose

only the parts of quarantine,

that weren't hurting anyone.
Maybe this has something

to do with the moon.

If the answer is a hot bath,
I might have a chance.

A voice in my head says, hear me out:

"What if you are actually a terrible person?
What if you are the personification

of the aftermath of a popped pimple?

What if all the stories in you
don't go together? What if they do

and everything is your fault?"

I remember to meditate, lock in on one point
of a leaf on a plant; the temperature

of the dishwater instead of 2014; get real small

so I have an affect on no one. Delight
must be the buzz she was talking about,

when she told me I could escape by staying.

Girls Rule Summer Camp

The men have ears so wide open, we string their heads together
like summer camp bracelets. Each of us wears our crush's name;
they all say *Me*. I eat my dinner at a turntable not spinning; everyone
wants to sit next to me. The men chew with their mouths closed.
When my heart breaks, there is a thunderstorm party and no one goes
outside. All of the umbrellas are padlocked shut. Everyone takes the batteries
out of their watches until I am ready to speak. When I cry over a minor
inconvenience, it is a lazy river and it is allowed to be. I fill a cooler
with fruit beer, tie one end to a raft shaped like a flamingo and the other
to a gust of glitter. I take bubbly gulps until I am tipsy and sunburnt
and playing footsie with my inner tube friends. I am proudly spilling
out of a string bikini. The men sit on the bank, don't touch anyone.
I recite poetry and the men don't think to tell me what I meant to say, they sit
criss-cross applesauce with their eyes closed, feeding on my experience
like it is sacramental bread. I am a gospel choir that the men hope does an encore.
I sit on a lawn chair and watch the season end; its beds respectfully stripped,
no comments about anyone's body swept under the rugs, all of the credit
put back where it came from. I wave to the men and tell them
it was a good summer. They lap up my praise like pets. I speak
and the men listen.

Church of the Big Sads

The Big Sads knock right on by the NO SOLICITATION sign
on the door and we cancel our dinner plans, offer
them a seat at the island. They open a hollowed out book
and start quoting scripture about people we miss
having fun without us. One of them spins
Mom's voicemail greeting on the record player. They remind us
to take the blame, ask to use the bathroom, piss in the kitchen sink.
The Big Sads take God out of the disco ball, they kick the dog,
ask about our afterlife plans. I run a bath to drown them out,
put eucalyptus oil and salt in my holy water.

The farmer's market next to the school shooting school opens

Next weekend, if you want to come with us, I want to pick
up a jar of that salty peanut butter and a green juice. I want
to buy produce to feed my in-laws when they are in town
and fresh flowers to say something about being the kind
of person who has fresh flowers at the start of the weekend.
Where I come from, we feed people. "Even my mother cared
that way," I laugh. My children are picky, but not bulletproof.
This is not hopeful, this is devastatingly routine: being so cavalier
that we share the parking lot with the swim meet and think nothing
of it. We made it to another Saturday,
almost to summer break.

Apalachee High School

School is back in session, we can hear it
in the breaking news. Every mother
in the posted text message screenshot
thought it wouldn't happen to her.
Inbox down to single digits,
coffee down to the ice,
cubicle, chime, pavement, screaming
her child's name, a violent prayer
to be one of the lucky ones.
That kind of emergency is a cancer
in their blood. She is rewired,
unwound, tangled in the barbs
of hope. Whatever child she finds
is forever different from the life
she imagined for them.
It becomes a regimen
the way we start to recognize
the magazine of their faces.

To the man driving with a sticker on his truck that says "BAN NARCAN"

Survival of the fittest is dead.
I want to be soft.

Burnout Diary

There I am on the way to the bathtub
justifying the exhaustion after a 60-hour week
of even better than my best, right? No one asked me
to say a word; over-explanation is a sign of trauma.
When I say "thank you for letting me alone", I'm fawning
"your body is nothing to weep about" to my mother.

Every Friday, I cry. Every Monday, I curl my hair.
If I stay in the water long enough, will they understand
why I need to be here in the first place? I get out,
an inconvenience to myself; not made to sit still; my grandma
at her machine hemming pants in 3AM's deep basement creaks and hum.
The men are always the drunkest at the party while I am checking
the window panes for spinach in my teeth. My therapist keeps telling me
how to work less and I keep telling her I understand
and then the body ache of burnout gnaws at the nape of my neck.
I wonder if my therapist is allowed to get sick of me.
Sometimes I get sick of myself on her behalf. I still don't know how I feel
about the way they have figured out how to make us faster; angry?

Yearning? Running full speed on my bare feet through the city?
It seems like everyone I'm trying to keep up with
has longer legs than mine. The finish is a line

from a song that's been stuck in my head.

Grief Is My Grandmother's Good Side

Grief knocks at the door and I am a wet lather.
I smudge a palmprint across the sweating
mirror, wrap myself in the towel that I forgot to bring

to the bathroom, puddle to the creak of the door,
open it to an empty stoop and the echoing doorbell
of his cologne asking me if I have changed my oil.

My grandfather named his only daughter after the lowest value
a coin comes in and it shows. He fathered and fathered
and died to my mother five years before he died; he died for so long.

Five days left, I can remember his deathbed. His bare chest treeline of bones,
his gums and all of the white capped bottles, *I want to go*, we screamed
at each other. Grief drove me home the day that I was brave enough

to show up, the day of grateful regret — two hours in a stitched together Ford
that did indeed need an oil change. Grief, in velvet and jewels. Grief,
a refrigerator covered in invitations with plus one you no longer have. Grief,

my old friend, it is truly terrible to see you unannounced every time, but also —
I called my grandmother. She told me about how she ate his favorite lunch
across from a framed photo of him standing next to his T-bird convertible,

a different picture but same ritual that she does on my birthday
since I moved out West. My high ponytail
and his arms on my shoulders in a Polaroid frame

before I became complicated.
My grandfather gave me the gift to exist as a girl in my baby teeth
and charm. My grandmother puts his memory in every gap and it fills.

She says he is somewhere watching over me. I do not believe that,
but I'm happy for her if she does.
Grief, with your painted claws and high heels;

You are the love of his life's good side.

Generational Joy

I've experienced the joy of choosing the rightest size Tupperware
for my leftovers so I am capable of this. I inhale October and the yellows

are more yellow, weep because I am laughing hard. I fell in love
with a man who always remembers to check for dings on the rental car

before we leave the lot. I let myself remember the snowglobe collection
in my purple teenage bedroom where I was very sad,

but loved the way they said *settle*. I notice that my two-year-old
doesn't eat the peach skin and I share slices with her.

Children should be noticed. I speak kindness to her
that my mother never spoke to me. I forgive the worst people

I have ever met. Sometimes, I sit in the bath
for so long I turn into soup and maybe I will never be a fulltime poet

or have a good mom or pay off my student loans,
but I do have the softest bed sheets.

My grandmother used to make the bed with me still in it,
the breeze pouring the sheer milk of the curtains into my cup.

She would pretend not to see
me, a lump giggling in the feathers.

She would say that she has to make her bed everyday
because if she dies, what would people think

of a crumble. Snickers and tells me this is also why I should
always wear clean underwear, in case of a car accident.

My grandmother smells like fabric softener and lipstick
and still dreams of my grandfather even after his gruesome death,

a treeline of sternum and credit card debt, wakes up and smells the ink
from their print shop on the pillow. You can see her teeth marks

in the butter bread and her only child is an empty stomach, a language
she does not speak. I call her from the train platform and the tragedies

of it all do not answer. She tells me how she made 6 quarts of soup
for the church, the volunteer firefighters are swooning for her

chocolate peanut butter cake, she is caught up on her yardwork,
she pays her credit card bill within two days of it coming in

the mail, makes a joke about the shape of her body that is outdated
and still endearing, tells me a man at bingo said she was the prettiest

girl in Newmanstown when she was younger, laughs and says
"that's not saying much," but still tells me; tells me she lost a lot

in the stock market, but never had it in her hand so, "no big deal."
She takes a walk every day and waves to people on porches, knows

their children's names, tells me not to worry so much. What she is
saying is there will always be all of the shit that has happened to us,

even if we do the good work, but there will be joys,
passed down from our grandmothers, the taste of them coating our teeth.

Dirty Monopoly

Grandma has always been good at games
played around a card table, dark cold outside,
snack plates appearing like magic.

They told me they were playing Dirty Monopoly. Dirty
meant that they grumbled "shit" and "motherfucker"
under their breath and accused everyone of cheating

while they were accused right back.
I would giggle from the bench we shared
while she made jokes about the space she took up

and let me bark her dog across the board.
Today, in a sad gap on the phone,
I told her there were good times, too,

back then. Like Dirty Monopoly.
It wasn't all mashed potatoes on the Thanksgiving wall and look at us now—
my daughter told me she knows what *archipelago* means and proves it,

says the kids think it's funny to mispronounce *butte*, but she doesn't.
My grandmother tells me that when she gets to the obits, she counts
the number of people older than her and the number of people younger.

Yesterday she was 13-7.

Pelt

It's not hard because you're bad at it.
It's hard because it is difficult:
being a body with a person inside of it.
We all got buttons.
Everybody's got a strong suit
and they are spun up
hula hoopin' and hollerin'
about 'em. Yesterday, I was trying
my damndest not to fall asleep
and tonight, I'll pray to the ceiling fan
and reruns of Law & Order. Thinking
about all the ways I could fall to bits
while Mercury is in retrograde
is not preparedness, it is anxiety.
That's the definition and I am
a dictionary of a woman, secure
in her goodness. I didn't come out
of the box like this. Everytime I see
a kid in a mud puddle and a parent
taking a photo of it smiling, I want
to give them both a kiss.
When Wilder washes the dishes,
our kitchen becomes shoreline.
You have to pretend kids are being helpful
so they learn what it feels like. I started
collecting marbles (again); still remember what it's like
having them strewn under the bed
for the monsters to teethe on.
I can't tell if we are talking to each other
or the dogs are barking. These conversations
spotlit around the kitchen island, fire
extinguisher on our tongue, to act
in spite of what tried to kill, the grace
of a taxidermist.

In Which the Woman in the Woods Learns to Make Coffee the Inconvenient Way

We should all be doing this more –
waking up in close proximity
to the steps in a meadow,
not holding back on the good

butter, the pen sliding
out of my hand. I wipe it
on my flannel, hang
my flannel on a branch

near a tree that can see
me naked. What luxury
lies in opting out, in sleeping
in. I can see how God

got this proud, I've lost track
of the rules around that,
but I'm happy she won
if this is what we get. This morning,

I looked for a snake
to see if I was still afraid
and I don't think I would
have been as much. Maybe

they have the right
idea, diluting their contact.
In their own way, rich,
staying warm.

Self Portrait of My Kitchen as Myself

Who is that lady

in the microwave reflecting?

Drinking more tea with honey

and lemon, coffee and cream

in the disco sun glitter;

listening to the velcro shards

of early 2000s pop punk love songs

and putting things in the mailbox.

The salty bomb of an olive & a glass of wine,

a bushel of myself planted on the windowsill,

drama at the neighbor's house

like before they had TV. I have enough

curiosity for a million people.

Between the Dentist and the Diagnosis

The internet tells me not to say "on the spectrum" and
the internet tells me to say "a person with autism" and
I will say the right thing to love the right people however

they want to be loved and what I know is that my daughter
is nine years old and when we go to a place with too much
music on the walls, she finds a blank corner, writes a book

on being tired. Ink drains from the fringe of her lashes to under
her eyes and I read the hourglass of it and become electric, become
more her mother, become static, but not static like still,

static like hair on balloon and spark on sweater and touched
like a
fuck you, do not.

My therapist asks me how activated
I am when I talk about fists and returned letters, not electric
like that. Electric like crawl back into me,

clip into my heartbeat, I am here to pedal you.
I will learn any language to help the world speak to you.
We go to the dentist and the hygienist asks over the volume

of your squirm if we have a diagnosis and I reach
into my pocket throat for the exact change and I am
a few cents short, but we are figuring it out together

and I am excited and ready, electric.

To My Mother Who I Am Disappointed In
An Ode to My Daughter's Taste in Music

She and I agree that the Jennifer Owens cover of Vampire is almost maybe
possibly better than the original. I swing her little sister around the kitchen

until I am out of breath from This Is Why by Paramore, both of us pogo stick
through the chorus. Today, for the first time in the car, she showed me a song

that I hadn't heard before that *she* has been listening to and it wasn't horrible
and listen, being proud is rock and roll, being tender and patient is metal as fuck.

She started building Spotify playlists, tells me every time a friend likes them.
She is getting down to Big by Tank & the Bangas and Freedia and I am, too!

I make a playlist every month, have for years thanks to a friend
who taught me not to forget the ages I've been along the way. Getting ready

for middle school Valentines Day, her crush twinkling in our giggle conversation
like champagne bubbles in a comic book, we listen to the one from February of last year.

I know her in a way my mother never knew me, but I wanted her to.
The venn diagram of neurodivergence and childhood trauma is she and I

kneading dough in the kitchen. You would still be so critical
like when you told me I couldn't sing, my favorite song blaring in the back

of the 1998 cherry red Dodge Neon that you drove off the lot
the year of my first chorus solo. You loved when The Steve Miller Band said

"really love your peaches, wanna shake your tree"
so much that you own the whole song in my head.

Do you turn the dial when you think of me? I don't when I think of you.
I wonder what you remember. I want to remember Lucy

on a snowy Saturday afternoon singing What's Up by 4 Non-Blondes,
my go-to karaoke song. Every time I freak out

about generational cycles and turning into you, my therapist
(who has a cross-stitch of Lady Gaga in her office) reminds me

that I've gotten this far. In seven years, I'll be older
than I ever knew my mother to be. She's not dead,

but she is gone and I have pierced more juice boxes with my short straws
than she ever did. To see a person develop a taste in music is a holy experience

that I devour in my children. I could never become you
with this much lyric in my guts.

Happy Buzzcut

This isn't a suicide note,
but if it were, read it
to my mother. Don't bother
with the mail, she isn't checking
the box. How could she be? *Right?*
I've been sending postcards
instead of letters to spare her
the effort of opening up.
Tell her I didn't consent to being born.
Tell her that to be abandoned is to have
a million tiny volcanoes stuck in your teeth.
A woo-woo stranger on the internet
told me hair holds memories.
I didn't fact check them, but it's plausible,
so when I go bottle rocket,
my head goes matchstick. My love
cleans up my edges wearing a headlamp,
nursing my wounds. When you read this to her,
don't let her be keyboard tapping away
in a cloud of Camel blue box.
She should have to pick this up
ten toes down, carry what she has done;
me in the bathroom
with a number three clipper guard
instead of celebrating
her birthday.

What Healing Tastes Like

Good Love accidentally sets the coffee pot to brew at 7:00PM
and I find the carafe with my nose; pour it into two mason jars

and feed it to the fridge without skipping a beat. Unclenched jaw,
mouthful of solve. I am a playground

dirt face with a head of feral knots and I'm growing
into my big teeth. Why do people say 'I'm *just* a teenage girl'?

There was nothing just about it.
I microdose rest by buying sheet masks

and if that's the best I can do, sobeit. Unfortunately,
it's true what they say about drinking water

and eating fruit and knowing what to call God.
It's hard for everyone,

so buy the good butter.

Springtime in Colorado

They say if you don't like the weather here, wait five minutes.
May is my hardest month.
It is the Grand Canyon on the calendar
of the good things that have happened; it hails.
In Colorado, the tulips are put to sleep under snow surprise
and she is on the east coast opening the mailbox in the rain,
picking up the phone and calling me back, but sometimes,
I get to hold a pair of sugar grub hands up to hang by the sill
and wait for their eyes to welcome their gasp, a stained glass window
stand off with the sky. My favorite version of the story
is when the clouds catch the sun, turn the bright dark into a color net.
We get distracted by the fascinating ordinary
and when we return to the window, we do so to a weary exhale
of monochrome glow. The clock is a scowl, returned to sender,
planted seconds bloom into these years of making it work.
Making it work is infinite.
I made it to the other side of the rainbow,
a home out of twigs and lint, made up my mind to celebrate
Mother's Day, made her birthday cake.
May is my hardest month,
but on the brightside look – it's Rainbow Season.

Spoon Theory

This is the summer I delete the apps
listen to whole albums
sprawled X-marks-the-spot across the floor;
check a book out of the library
because the cover is an illustration of two middle fingers;
watch a cucumber grow in real time.

I make believe David Letterman is my dream dad
and if *he* called me, I *would* pick up the phone
and he would tell me he was proud of me.
What if everybody likes me
and I do too?
Look at the garden.

She pretends she can't and she does anyway.
The reality is, we are not that far removed
from when people could smoke in the grocery store
and the truth is, I was wrong about everything
and not only do my children have no idea,
but they wouldn't believe it if they did.

So, sure – there is a version of myself
that's an ice cube thrown into a blizzard
and my mother's nose is on my face,
but I braid their hair like I'm praying
to the god of my own intuition.
I know that I have to teach my children

to be kind. This summer, I'm saying no
to everything. Send 'em to voicemail before they even call.
I got a bouquet of boundaries in the kitchen
and three baby birds in a wreath on my front door.
Someday, I will be ancient as the ocean,
but until then, I'll keep practicing not being mean to people.

Fortunately, not everything is up to me,
but the spoons I keep in my mouth are.

RSVP: Maybe

If the Sumerians had known that I would have to make
a post-putting-our-children-to-bedtime Google event
wearing nothing but a trenchcoat called 'Scrabble'
to be sure that we conserved enough energy to make love,
I do not think they would have invented the calendar.

Imagine their horror in finding out our time
was something that could be taken. Imagine
them pricking themselves on the point of a sundial
and realizing it could be called *weapon*.
When they invented the calendar,
deadlines didn't exist, no one had to say *hurry*.

Upside Down Envy

When it comes to giving, you can trace my reach all the way
to fish born with lanterns growing out of their minds
and when it comes to giving, you are a puddle of spit.

Our grandma says that whatever you give comes back to you
tenfold and I don't understand what I am doing wrong

with my elbows, how my boomerangs keep getting caught
in your teeth. When you chew, it is silent, contained. I am a mess
of experiencing every tang. There have been years that I am

a sink full of crusted dishes. This is not to say
that I want what you want because nowhere feels like home

as much as home does these days.
I pin the blue ribbon on that in between therapy sessions
and emotional support bathtubs. I want to forgive my sister

in this poem, I want to find the words to say
that when it comes to loving her, I am doing my best

except recently I've decided to stop
doing my best and start doing
exactly however well I am doing.

Vitamins

She runs into the kitchen and yells,
Kuvo the dog hasn't had his vitamins and neither have I,

pulls a stool to the cabinet, grubby knuckles
puckered with determination,

hot potatoes two plastic bottles to me and pants
anticipation as I push and twist the childlock tops,

stick my hand in the top, she megaphones
a desperate *NO*

I CAN DO IT, pulls a 90 degree day ball of gummies out
and she picks two before I can even remind her.

She hole in ones each one at her mouth, reaches her palm up
for the big button of a dog supplement. I hand her one and she tells me

he gets two.
My parents may not have ever taught me

to care for anything, anything,
but look at us – figuring it out anyway.

Post Mortem

On my birthday, I spend a concerning amount of time thinking
about who is going to find my notebooks after I die. I hope
there are hundreds, maybe a thousand, of them waiting
waggishly to be found. I hope that the readers remark
on the covers and look up the names of workshop
facilitators and read their poems and remember
their books in another dusty box and I hope
that they understand that my angriest journal
entries exist mostly to get it out of me,
not always to be the truest version
of a person; which reminds me,
this year I want to write more
odes.

Good Love

There are hardly any fathers on my pages, but here
you are. That time you said you were so sad

you wanted to put pizza rolls on your pizza,
I've never loved you more. I wouldn't say

that I am lovesick on the road, but I would say I miss
your toothbrush in my mouth. All the bad parents

I know blame their children for being born,
but not us. It's not that I think everyone hates me,

it's that I don't think I'm anyone's favorite,
except yours. We aren't in love in the combustible way

that the couple on the airplane are tonguing
across the aisle. We used to be, but now you are

all I think about as I chase the Pacific up the coast
of Northern California. When I make it home late,

you've dimmed my bedside light to 10% –
enough to find your hand under the covers.

Instructions to My Midlife Crisis

Look for a trampoline bouncing with summer moths,
for snow angels flapping in the bed so the dog can't lay down.
You see the yellow tricycle adopted by ants? The evolution of pinky fingers?
A whole garden grown by accident?
See the corn cobs on the tablescape
and toilet paper combed by the tree branches in the front yard
of my burnout's house.
Yes, we are disagreeing about where to park the car.
Yes, I have a fear of clipping toenails
and wonder if I ever should have been a mother.
Over there: $7 coffee and four disintegrating tissues
on the front seat after therapy.
Out front, the mailman is leaving an angry note about the bees
and to the left is me:
pacing the bedroom,
birthing a poem,
a woman in the bathtub
again.

We Found the Night Routine

All week, we've been finding math problems
in the toaster. Those kids: unapologetic
as spoons under the faucet.

When I was 11, I dreamt
of giving my dad the finger,
now Lucy is in her bedroom,

ankle deep in mess, bird perched
on fist behind the door pretending
with my own mother's hand

to do the same to us.
The baby isn't mad, but
she is practicing how to be

and by this point in the day we are
the crouch of a shrimp shell eating
shredded cheese over the kitchen sink.

Monday was the bottom of a tornado, today
was untangling a slinky. After two stories,
we turn on the crickets, say goodnight

to the yard flamingos and the neighborhood.
We two puddles dribbling
into bed, gnawing peach rings,

no hare, only tortoise, our minds: moving
vans circling the block; we'll come back
tomorrow. We love it here.

Gratitudes

Thank you to the people who gave me their time and attention, reading various iterations of this book as it morphed into its final form: Desiree Dallagiacomo, Olivia Dudding Rodriguez, Chrissy Croft, Holly Hosterman, Cara Morris, Sam Slupski, and Megan Falley. Your feedback, kindness, and patience live on these pages.

Many of these poems were born in spaces held by Megan Falley, Andrea Gibson, Jon Sands, Buddy Wakefield, and Desiree Dallagiacomo. They were scribbled in crayon on the backs of coloring pages, scrawled on receipts in the parking lot of my therapist's office, typed across approximately 17 different Apple Notes, and pieced together on the RTD N-Line, in a couple of airports, and more than one bathtub.

Endless gratitude to my dear friend and editor, Devin Devine, who I had the joy of snacking with, drinking tea with, and reading poems with – the best way to experience a person, I believe. Our weekend in Portland, made possible by this book, remains one of the sweetest gifts.

Cindy, so much of the clarity I've found carries a whisper of your voice. Thank you for teaching me, for being proud of me, and most of all – for giggling through the hardest parts with me.

In every phase of life, I've had the extraordinary luck of finding best friends who know how to love people well. Nicole, Laura, Julie, my Sheilas, Cayte, Rainier— each of you has given me tools to make better choices and a softer place to land. Thank you for seeing me in a positive light, calling me on my shit, and being my family.

If you know me, you know I couldn't get through a list of gratitude without mentioning the dogs – especially my sweet girls, Annie and Mud, and my lil' freak boy, Disco.

Mem, if you read this book, I hope you see that the love stories outweigh everything else. That is your and Papa's doing.

Lucy, by the time this book is in your hands, you'll be a teenager – a wonderful and bewildering thing to be. Every day, you bring me face-to-face with adolescence in a way that has healed parts of me I thought were beyond repair. You show up in these poems because you are art and an artist, and I am so grateful to know and love you.

Wilder, while I wrote these acknowledgments, you sprayed an entire bottle of detangler in your hair. Throughout your early childhood, you breastfed through pandemic workshops, bounced on my knee, watercolored, and collected rocks while I wrote. You have been a constant presence in this process, which is a magical and generous thing to share with someone. Love you, Tink.

And possibly most of all, Trevor—thank you for the mental space it takes to be an artist while parenting, for living differently with me, for never saying no to figuring out our path, and for accepting me as I am and as I am not. Loved you then, love you still. Always have, always will.

Lastly, to you, the Reader, I hope you found a shadow of yourself somewhere in these pages. I found myself a million times while writing them. If there is anything I hope you carry with you, it's this: if you focus on how you want to feel and move unabashedly in the direction of that feeling, you just might look around one day and find yourself in an entirely different place than where you started.

Abby Hosterman (she/her) is a poet and parent to two humans and four dogs, originally from Pennsylvania and now based in Denver, CO. Her work has appeared in The Rumpus, Chaotic Merge Magazine, BarBar, and more. A multiyear finalist for the Write Bloody Jack McCarthy Book Prize, she has also been recognized as a finalist for the Adams County Poet Laureate Residency and nominated for a Best of the Net Award in Poetry. Abby's poetry explores the complexities of motherhood, parental estrangement, and trauma recovery. She is the author of two self-published chapbooks: *What Ails You* (2020) and *Mom Shit* (2024). *Burnout Diary* is her debut full-length collection.